FINDING YOUR PASSION

A GUIDE TO DISCOVERING YOUR LIFE'S PURPOSE

DR. JAGADEESH PILLAI

Made with ♥ on the Notion Press Platform
www.notionpress.com

|| **Dedicated to all wisdom seekers around the World** ||

ନ

Contents

Contents

PRAYER

"Om Bhadram Karnebhih Shrunuyaama DevaahBhadram Pashyemaakshabhiryajatraah SthiraiirangaistushtuvaamsastanoobhihVyashema Devahitam YadaayuhSwasti Na Indro VridhashravaahSwasti Nah Pooshaa VishwavedaahSwasti Nastaarkshyo ArishtanemihSwasti No Brihaspatir DadhaatuOm Shantih, Shantih, Shantih"

The literal meaning of this mantra is: OM. O Gods! Let us hear auspicious words from our ears. O reverent Gods! Let us behold propitious visions from our eyes, let our organs and body be stable, healthy, and strong. Let us do that which is pleasing to the gods in the life span allotted to us. May Indra, inscribed in the scriptures, bring us fortune! May Pushan, the knower of the world, grant us prosperity! May Trakshya, who vanquishes enemies, bestow us with blessings! May Brihaspati bring us success!
OM Peace, Peace, Peace.

About The Author

Dr. Jagadeesh Pillai is a renowned Guinness World Record holder, writer, and researcher hailing from Varanasi, also known as the abode of Lord Shiva. With a Ph.D. in Vedic Science and a range of creative ideas and achievements, he is a true polymath. He is the author of more than 100 books including Research Publications. Although his roots can be traced back to Kerala, the people of Varanasi hold him in high regard and affectionately consider him one of their own.

In 1998, Dr. Pillai was offered a job at Banaras Hindu University, but he left the position after only two months to pursue greater goals in life. He believed that in order to study Indian scriptures and engage in other creative endeavours, he needed to retire from the daily grind of working solely for money at a young age.

He started an export business from scratch, using the knowledge he had gained from a previous job in the industry. His intelligence and unique approach to business led to great success in a short period of time, earning him more in just a decade and a half than he would have in a lifetime working in a government job. Upon the passing of Dr. APJ Abdul Kalam, Dr. Pillai decided to leave the business and dedicate himself to reading, studying, researching, and experimenting.

During his tenure in the export business, Dr. Pillai traveled to over 16 countries, gaining valuable insight and experiencing the world and life in detail.

Dr. Pillai has achieved four Guinness World Records in the following subjects:

"Script to Screen" - In this record, Dr. Pillai produced and directed an animation film within the shortest time possible, breaking the previous record set by Canadians. He has also received numerous national and international awards and recognitions for this achievement.

Longest Line of Postcards - For this record, Dr. Pillai created a line of 16,300 postcards on the occasion of the 163rd anniversary of Indian Postal Day. The event also included a questionnaire about the Indian flag.

Largest Poster Awareness Campaign - Dr. Pillai designed an awareness campaign on the subject of "Beti Bachao - Beti Padhao" (Save the Girl Child - Educate the Girl Child) to achieve this record.

Largest Envelope - In tribute to the Indian Prime Minister's "Make in India" initiative, Dr. Pillai created a 4000 square meter envelope using waste paper to achieve this record.

Attempted - **70000 Candles on a 210 kg Cake** - To celebrate the 70th Indian Independence Day, Dr. Pillai attempted to light 70,000 candles on a 210 kg cake, which was recorded in World Records India.

Attempted - **Documentary on Dhamek Stupa of Sarnath in 17 Languages** - Dr. Pillai attempted to create a documentary on the Dhamek Stupa of Sarnath, dubbing it in 17 different languages. The result of this attempt is currently awaiting confirmation from the Guinness World Records.

Dr. Pillai is skilled in teaching the Bhagavad Gita, a Hindu scripture, and is popular among young people. He has helped many young people improve their lives through his motivational teachings.

In addition to teaching, he has composed and sung numerous Sanskrit Bhajans and patriotic songs.

He has also written and directed several short films and documentaries for awareness campaigns, and has volunteered with the police in both UP and Kerala to spread awareness about various issues through videos and photography.

Incredibly, he has produced and directed over 100 documentaries about the city of Varanasi, all on his own.

He has also helped and guided more than 25 boys and girls to achieve world records through creative and innovative methods. He is a multifaceted person who uses his intellect and the blessings given to him by God to excel in various areas. He is both a teacher and a student, always learning and teaching, and is able to master any subject he comes across.

He is a selfless social activist and motivational speaker who has overcome struggles and failures to become a successful and enthusiastic individual with a rich life experience.

In addition to his work with the Bhagavad Gita, he is also an efficient Tarot card reader, Astro-Vastu consultant, and a talented singer and composer. He has sung the entire Ram Charita Manas and Bhagavad Gita in his own compositions, and has sung the phrase "Lokah Samastha Sukhino Bhavantu" in 50 different languages. He is currently working on a detailed and scientific study of Vedas, Upanishads, Puranas, and the Bhagavad Gita. He has also composed and sung the Hanuman Chalisa and Gayatri Mantra in 108 and 1008 different compositions, respectively.

Awards - Four Times Guinness World Records, Winner of Mahatma Gandhi Vishwa Shanti Puraskar, Mahatma Gandhi Global Peace Ambassador, Kashi Ratna Award, Dr. APJ Abdul Kalam Motivational Person of the Year 2017, Mother Teresa Award, Indira Gandhi Priyadarshini Award, Bharat Vikas Ratna Award, Udyog Ratna Award, Vigyan Prasar Award, Poorvanchal Ratn Samman.

Preface

We all have a unique purpose in life, but sometimes it can be difficult to find. That's why I wrote "Finding Your Passion: A Guide to Discovering Your Life's Purpose". This book is designed to help you uncover your true passions and find the path that will lead you to a life of fulfillment and joy.

In this book, I provide practical advice and exercises to help you identify your passions and develop a plan to pursue them. I also discuss the importance of self-reflection and how to use it to gain clarity and insight into your life's purpose. Additionally, I provide tips on how to stay motivated and inspired as you work towards achieving your goals.

This book is for anyone who is looking to find their true purpose in life. Whether you're just starting out or have been searching for a while, this book will provide you with the tools and guidance you need to find your passion and live a life of purpose.

I hope that this book will help you to discover your true passions and find the path that will lead you to a life of fulfillment and joy. With the right guidance and dedication, you can find your passion and live a life of purpose.

I

What is Passion and How to Find It

Passion is an emotion that can be difficult to define, but it is something that everyone can experience. It is a powerful force that can drive us to pursue our dreams and goals, and it can be the source of great joy and fulfillment. But how do we find our passion?

The first step in finding your passion is to take a step back and reflect on what you truly enjoy doing. Think about the activities that bring you joy and make you feel alive. It could be anything from playing a sport to painting to writing. Once you have identified the activities that bring you joy, you can start to explore them further.

The next step is to take action. Start by researching the activity that you are interested in and learning more about it. Talk to people who are already involved in the activity and ask them questions. This will help you gain a better understanding of the activity and what it takes to be successful.

Once you have a better understanding of the activity, it is time to start taking action. Start by setting small goals and working towards them. This will help you stay motivated and focused on your passion. As you progress, you may find that you need to make adjustments to your goals or even change your focus. This is all part of the process of finding your passion.

Finally, it is important to remember that passion is something that you must nurture. It is not something that you can find overnight. It takes time and effort to develop and grow. As you continue to pursue your passion, you will find that it will become a part of who you are and will bring you great joy and fulfillment.

Finding your passion is an exciting journey that can lead to a life of purpose and fulfillment. It is important to take the time to reflect on what you truly enjoy doing and to take action to pursue it. With dedication and perseverance, you can find your passion and use it to create a life of joy and fulfillment.

"Your passion is the compass that guides you to your purpose in life."

ᘓ

II

Knowing Yourself a Foundation for Finding Passion

Knowing yourself is the foundation for finding your passion in life. It is essential to understand who you are, what you value, and what you want out of life in order to discover your purpose. This chapter will explore the importance of self-awareness and how it can help you find your passion.

Self-awareness is the ability to recognize and understand your own emotions, thoughts, and behaviors. It is the foundation of emotional intelligence and is essential for personal growth and development. When you are self-aware, you can better understand your strengths and weaknesses, as well as your values and goals. This knowledge can help you make decisions that are in line with your values and goals, and ultimately lead you to your passion.

Self-awareness also helps you to recognize and understand the emotions of others. This is important because it allows you to empathize with others and build meaningful relationships. When you understand the emotions of those around you, you can better understand their perspectives and motivations. This can help you to better collaborate with others and work together to achieve a common goal.

In addition to understanding yourself and others, self-awareness can also help you to identify and manage stress. When you are aware of your emotions and reactions to stress, you can better manage them and prevent them from negatively impacting your life. This can help you to stay focused on your goals and stay motivated to pursue your passion.

Finally, self-awareness can help you to recognize and appreciate the beauty in life. When you are aware of your emotions and reactions to the world around you, you can better appreciate the small moments and find joy in the everyday. This can help you to stay positive and motivated to pursue your passion.

Self-awareness is essential for finding your passion in life. It helps you to understand yourself, others, and the world around you. It can help you to make decisions that are in line with your values and goals, build meaningful relationships, and increase your happiness and overall well-being. By developing self-awareness, you can become more confident, resilient, and better equipped to navigate the challenges of life. This can lead to greater success in personal and professional domains, as well as a more fulfilling life. Cultivating self-awareness requires patience, commitment, and a willingness to look inward, but the benefits are well worth the effort. By learning to understand yourself and others, you can unlock the secrets to a fulfilling life and take the first steps towards realizing your full potential.

"The journey to discovering your passion begins with self-reflection."

ꟽ

III

Making Connections Exploring Possible Passions

Once you have developed a strong sense of self-awareness and have a clearer understanding of your values, interests, and strengths, the next step is to start exploring potential passions and careers. This process of exploration can be overwhelming, but it is important to take the time to reflect on what you want to achieve and what you are truly passionate about.

Making connections and exploring new opportunities can be a great way to uncover potential passions and find the right path for you. Consider the following steps:

Talk to people who have jobs or careers that you find

interesting. Ask them about their experiences, what they like about their jobs, and what advice they have for someone who is interested in that field.

Take advantage of opportunities to try new things. Whether it's volunteering, taking a class, or attending a workshop, expanding your knowledge and experience will help you to uncover new passions and interests.

Consider your values and goals. What are you looking to achieve in your personal and professional life? Make sure that any potential passions align with your values and goals.

Utilize online resources to find information about different careers and industries. Look for forums and websites that allow you to connect with people who have similar interests and goals.

Network and attend events related to your potential passions. This will give you the opportunity to meet like-minded individuals and learn about different career paths in your field of interest.

Making connections and exploring new opportunities can be an exciting and valuable part of the journey towards finding your passion. By taking the time to reflect on your values, interests, and strengths, and by seeking out new experiences, you will be well on your way to discovering your life's purpose.

Finding your passion requires a combination of self-awareness and exploration. By taking the time to reflect on your values and interests, and by seeking out new experiences, you will be well on your way to finding the right path for you. With persistence and determination, you can uncover your true passions and live a fulfilling life.

"Your passion is the spark that ignites your purpose."

ꟸ

IV

Becoming an Expert Refining Your Passion

Becoming an expert in refining your passion is an important step in discovering your life's purpose. It requires dedication, focus, and a willingness to learn and grow. To become an expert, you must first identify your passion and then develop a plan to refine it.

Start by taking the time to reflect on what you are passionate about. Ask yourself questions such as: What do I enjoy doing? What do I find interesting? What do I want to learn more about? Once you have identified your passion, it is time to start refining it.

Begin by researching your passion. Read books, articles, and blogs related to your topic. Attend seminars and workshops to learn from experts in the field. Take classes or enroll in online courses to gain a deeper understanding of the subject.

Next, practice what you have learned. Put your knowledge into action by creating projects or participating in activities related to your passion. This will help you gain experience and develop your skills.

Finally, network with other professionals in the field. Connect with people who share your passion and learn from their experiences. This will help you stay motivated and inspired.

By taking the time to refine your passion, you will become an expert in the field. You will gain a deeper understanding of the subject and be able to use your knowledge to pursue your life's purpose. With dedication and hard work, you can become an expert in refining your passion and discover your life's purpose.

Networking with other professionals in your field is also a great way to build relationships and create opportunities for collaboration. By connecting with like-minded individuals, you can learn from their experiences, share your own insights, and stay up-to-date with the latest developments in the field. Furthermore, networking can also help you to identify potential mentors and role models, who can provide guidance and support as you navigate your career. And, it can also help you to expand your professional network and increase your visibility, which can lead to new and exciting opportunities. So, be proactive about networking and make the most of the opportunities to connect with others who share your passions and interests.

"The key to finding your passion is to explore what brings you joy."

V

Taking Action Implementing Your Passion

Taking action to implement your passion is an essential step in discovering your life's purpose. It can be daunting to take the plunge and start pursuing your dreams, but it is also incredibly rewarding. To help you get started, here are some tips for taking action and implementing your passion.

First, identify your passion.

What do you love to do? What activities bring you joy and fulfillment? Once you have identified your passion, it's time to take action. Start small and build up. You don't have to take on a huge project right away. Start with something manageable and achievable.

Second, create a plan.

Once you have identified your passion, create a plan for how you will pursue it. What steps will you take? What resources do you need? What timeline will you follow? Having a plan will help you stay focused and motivated.

Third, take action.

Once you have a plan, it's time to take action. Start by setting small, achievable goals. Break down your plan into manageable tasks and set deadlines for yourself. Taking action will help you stay on track and make progress towards your goals.

Fourth, stay motivated.

Pursuing your passion can be difficult and it's easy to get discouraged. To stay motivated, set yourself up for success. Celebrate your successes, no matter how small. Reward yourself for completing tasks and reaching milestones.

Finally, don't give up. It's easy to get discouraged when things don't go as planned. Don't give up. Keep going and stay focused on your goals. With dedication and hard work, you can achieve your dreams.

Taking action to implement your passion is an important step in discovering your life's purpose. It can be intimidating to take the plunge, but it is also incredibly rewarding. By identifying your passion, creating a plan, taking action, staying motivated, and never giving up, you can make progress towards achieving your goals and living a life of purpose.

One of the best ways to take action towards your passion is to start making connections with people who share your interests and goals. This can include attending events, joining clubs or organizations, connecting with others online, and reaching out to individuals who inspire you. These connections can provide you with the support, encouragement, and guidance you need to turn your passion into a reality.

It is also important to explore all possible avenues of your passion. For example, if your passion is writing, consider writing in different genres, such as fiction, non-fiction, poetry, or screenwriting. Or, if your passion is photography, experiment with different styles and techniques to see what resonates with you. By exploring your passion in different ways, you can broaden your understanding of what your passion truly is, and find new and exciting ways to pursue it.

It is also essential to be open-minded and flexible as you make progress towards your goals. You may discover that your passion evolves and changes over time, and that is okay. Embrace the journey and be willing to try new things. The process of discovering your passion is not about arriving at a specific destination, but about exploring, learning, and growing along the way.

Making connections and exploring possible passions is an important step in discovering your life's purpose. By reaching out to others and exploring all the different facets of your passion, you can gain a deeper understanding of your interests and goals, and find the path that is right for you. With dedication, hard work, and a willingness to take risks, you can make your passion a reality and live a life of purpose.

"Your passion is the fuel that drives you to achieve your goals."

VI

Overcoming Blocks to Passion and Fulfillment

Finding your passion and achieving fulfillment can be a daunting task. Many of us struggle to identify our passions and to take the necessary steps to pursue them. This chapter of "Finding Your Passion: A Guide to Discovering Your Life's Purpose" will explore the common blocks to passion and fulfillment and provide strategies for overcoming them.

One of the most common blocks to passion and fulfillment is fear. Fear of failure, fear of the unknown, and fear of the future can all prevent us from taking the necessary steps to pursue our passions. To overcome this fear, it is important to focus on the present moment and to take small steps towards our goals. It is also important to remember that failure is a part of the learning process and that it is okay to make mistakes.

Another common block to passion and fulfillment is lack of motivation. It can be difficult to stay motivated when pursuing a passion, especially when the journey is long and difficult. To stay motivated, it is important to set realistic goals and to celebrate small successes along the way. It is also important to remember why you are pursuing your passion in the first place and to focus on the end goal.

Finally, a lack of resources can be a major block to passion and fulfillment. It can be difficult to pursue a passion when you don't have the necessary resources. To overcome this block, it is important to be creative and to look for alternative solutions. It is also important to reach out to your network and to ask for help when needed.

By recognizing and overcoming the common blocks to passion and fulfillment, we can take the necessary steps to pursue our passions and to achieve our goals. With dedication and perseverance, we can find our passion and live a life of fulfillment.

Here are some common blocks that can get in the way of pursuing your passion:

Fear of Failure - Many people are afraid of failing and not living up to their own or others' expectations. But it is important to remember that failure is a natural part of the process of growth and learning.

Lack of Self-Belief - Some individuals may not believe in themselves and their abilities to pursue their passions. This can lead to self-doubt and can be a major roadblock.

Limited Time and Resources - People often feel that they don't have the time or resources to pursue their passions. But with a little creativity and a lot of dedication, it is possible to overcome these limitations.

Resistance from Others - Sometimes friends, family, or even colleagues may not support your passion or goals. It's important to seek out supportive relationships and to have the confidence to follow your own path.

To overcome these blocks, it is essential to develop a growth mindset and to have a positive outlook on life. This involves embracing challenges, viewing failures as opportunities for growth, and focusing on the process of discovery. It is also important to have a support system, be it friends, family, or a mentor, who can encourage and motivate you on your journey.

Making connections and exploring possible passions is a critical step in finding your life's purpose. By being open to new experiences, seeking out supportive relationships, and overcoming common blocks, you can make progress towards living a life of fulfillment and purpose.

"The path to discovering your passion starts with understanding yourself."

ꕤ

VII

Harnessing Technology to Fuel Your Passion

Technology has become an integral part of our lives, and it can be used to help us discover our passions and purpose. In the book, "Finding Your Passion: A Guide to Discovering Your Life's Purpose," readers are provided with the tools and resources to help them harness technology to fuel their passions.

The book begins by exploring the concept of passion and how it can be used to drive our lives. It then delves into the various ways technology can be used to help us find our passions. From using online resources to explore our interests to utilizing social media to connect with like-minded individuals, the book provides readers with a comprehensive guide to using technology to fuel their passions.

The book also provides readers with tips and strategies for using technology to stay motivated and focused on their passions. It covers topics such as setting goals, creating a plan of action, and staying organized. Additionally, the book provides readers with advice on how to use technology to stay connected with their passions and how to use it to create meaningful relationships with others.

Finally, the book provides readers with a comprehensive guide to using technology to fuel their passions. It covers topics such as using technology to stay organized, setting goals, and creating a plan of action. Additionally, the book provides readers with advice on how to use technology to stay connected with their passions and how to use it to create meaningful relationships with others.

In conclusion, technology can be a powerful tool in helping us discover our passions and purpose. By utilizing technology, we can explore our interests, connect with like-minded individuals, stay motivated and focused, and ultimately achieve our goals. This book, "Finding Your Passion: A Guide to Discovering Your Life's Purpose," provides readers with a comprehensive guide to using technology to fuel their passions and achieve their life's purpose. Whether you're just starting on your journey of self-discovery or you're looking for ways to reignite your passions, this book has something for everyone. So, what are you waiting for? Take the first step today and start exploring your passions with the power of technology!

"Your passion is the bridge that connects you to your life's purpose."

VIII

Making a Life Building a Career Around Your Passion

Making a life and building a career around your passion is a rewarding and fulfilling experience. It can be a difficult journey, but with the right mindset and dedication, it is possible to achieve success.

The first step in making a life and building a career around your passion is to identify what it is that you are passionate about. This can be anything from a hobby to a profession. Once you have identified your passion, it is important to research the field and gain an understanding of the industry. This will help you to determine the best way to pursue your passion and create a career out of it.

The next step is to create a plan. This plan should include a timeline of when you want to achieve certain goals, as well as a budget for any necessary expenses. It is also important to consider the resources available to you, such as mentors, networking opportunities, and educational programs.

Once you have a plan in place, it is time to take action. This may involve taking classes, attending seminars, or even starting a business. It is important to remember that success does not happen overnight. It takes hard work and dedication to make a life and build a career around your passion.

Finally, it is important to stay motivated and focused on your goals. This can be done by setting small, achievable goals and celebrating each success. It is also important to remember to take time for yourself and enjoy the journey.

Making a life and building a career around your passion is a rewarding and fulfilling experience. With the right mindset, dedication, and a plan in place, it is possible to achieve success. By taking the time to identify your passion, research the field, create a plan, and take action, you can make a life and build a career around your passion. With hard work and dedication, you can make your dreams a reality.

"The secret to finding your passion lies in embracing your unique gifts."

ꕤ

IX

Finding Balance in Life and Career

Finding balance in life and career is essential for achieving success and fulfillment. In order to find balance, it is important to understand the importance of both work and leisure, and to create a plan that allows for both.

The first step in finding balance is to recognize the importance of both work and leisure. Work provides us with a sense of purpose and accomplishment, while leisure allows us to relax and recharge. It is important to recognize that both are essential for a healthy and fulfilling life.

The next step is to create a plan that allows for both work and leisure. This plan should include a schedule that allows for both. It is important to set aside time for both work and leisure, and to stick to the schedule. This will help to ensure that both are given the attention they deserve.

It is also important to recognize that balance is not a one-time event. It is an ongoing process that requires regular attention and adjustment. As life and career goals change, it is important to adjust the plan accordingly.

Finally, it is important to remember that balance is not just about work and leisure. It is also about taking care of oneself. This includes getting enough sleep, eating healthy, exercising, and taking time for self-care. All of these things are essential for achieving balance in life and career.

Finding balance in life and career is an important part of achieving success and fulfillment. By recognizing the importance of both work and leisure, creating a plan that allows for both, and taking care of oneself, it is possible to achieve balance and lead a fulfilling life.

Yes, balancing work and personal life is crucial for overall well-being and success. It involves setting priorities, setting boundaries, and taking care of one's physical and mental health. Achieving balance may require making changes to one's work schedule or finding ways to manage stress, but it is worth the effort to lead a happier, more fulfilling life.

"Your passion is the key to unlocking your potential."

ℬ

X

Life-Work Integration Combining Your Passions

Life-work integration is a concept that has become increasingly popular in recent years. It involves combining your passions and interests with your professional life in order to create a more meaningful and fulfilling career. This chapter will explore the concept of life-work integration and provide practical tips for combining your passions with your professional life.

Life-work integration is about more than just finding a job that pays the bills. It's about finding a career that is meaningful and fulfilling, and that allows you to pursue your passions and interests. It's about creating a life that is balanced and that allows you to make the most of your time and energy.

The first step in life-work integration is to identify your passions and interests. What do you enjoy doing? What do you find meaningful and fulfilling? What do you want to do with your life? Once you have identified your passions and interests, you can begin to explore ways to incorporate them into your professional life.

One way to do this is to look for jobs that align with your passions and interests. For example, if you are passionate about the environment, you may want to look for a job in the environmental sector. Or, if you are passionate about writing, you may want to look for a job in the publishing industry.

Another way to integrate your passions and interests into your professional life is to create your own business. This could involve starting a blog, launching an online store, or creating a consulting business. This is a great way to pursue your passions and interests while also making a living.

Finally, you can also look for ways to incorporate your passions and interests into your current job. For example, if you are passionate about writing, you may be able to write articles or blog posts for your company. Or, if you are passionate about the environment, you may be able to suggest ways to make your company more sustainable.

Life-work integration is a powerful concept that can help you create a sense of fulfillment and meaning in your career. By finding ways to align your work with your passions and interests, you can enjoy greater satisfaction and happiness in your personal and professional life. This can also bring new perspectives and creativity to your work, which can benefit both you and your organization. Overall, life-work integration is an important aspect of achieving balance and success in your career.

"The answer to discovering your passion lies within you."

ꕤ

XI

Managing Fear and Anxiety When Pursuing Your Passions

Fear and anxiety can be a major obstacle when it comes to pursuing your passions. It can be difficult to take the first step towards achieving your goals, especially when fear and anxiety are holding you back. However, with the right strategies, you can manage your fear and anxiety and take the steps necessary to pursue your passions.

One of the most important things to remember when managing fear and anxiety is to be kind to yourself. It is normal to feel scared or anxious when taking risks or trying something new. Acknowledge your feelings and give yourself permission to feel them. Remind yourself that it is okay to be scared and that you can still take action despite your fear.

Another important strategy for managing fear and anxiety is to break down your goals into smaller, more manageable steps. When you have a large goal, it can be overwhelming and intimidating. Breaking it down into smaller steps can make it seem more achievable and less daunting. Additionally, it can help you to focus on the progress you are making, rather than the end goal.

It is also important to practice self-care when managing fear and anxiety. Make sure to take time for yourself to relax and recharge. This could include activities such as yoga, meditation, or journaling. Additionally, make sure to get enough sleep and eat healthy meals. Taking care of your physical and mental health can help you to feel more capable of tackling your goals.

Finally, it is important to remember that fear and anxiety are normal and that you are not alone. Everyone experiences fear and anxiety at some point in their lives. It is important to reach out to friends and family for support and to talk to a mental health professional if needed.

Fear and anxiety can be a major obstacle when it comes to pursuing your passions, but with the right strategies, you can manage your fear and anxiety and take the steps necessary to achieve your goals. By being kind to yourself, breaking down your goals into smaller steps, and seeking support from friends, family, or a therapist, you can overcome your fears and anxiety.

It is also helpful to practice mindfulness, deep breathing,

and other stress-management techniques to calm your mind and reduce feelings of stress and anxiety. Additionally, education and learning about what triggers your fears can help you face them and work through them in a healthier and more effective manner. Remember, everyone experiences fear and anxiety at some point in their lives, and it is important to approach these emotions with self-compassion and a growth mindset. With time and persistence, you can overcome your fears and pursue your passions with confidence and determination.

"Your passion is the fire that lights the way to your destiny."

XII

Crafting a Life's Work Creating a Living Out of Your Passion

Pursuing your passion can be a daunting task, but it can also be incredibly rewarding. It takes dedication, hard work, and a willingness to take risks. But if you're willing to put in the effort, you can create a life and a career out of your passion.

The first step in crafting a life's work is to identify your passion. What do you love to do? What activities bring you joy and fulfillment? Once you've identified your passion, you can begin to explore ways to make it into a career.

Start by researching the field you're interested in. Learn about the industry, the job market, and the skills you'll need to succeed. You may need to take classes or gain certifications to make yourself more marketable.

Next, create a plan. What steps do you need to take to make your passion into a career? What resources do you need? What goals do you need to set? Make sure to set realistic goals and timelines.

Once you have a plan in place, it's time to start taking action. Reach out to people in the industry, network, and look for opportunities. Don't be afraid to take risks and try new things. You may need to start small and work your way up, but don't give up.

Finally, remember to take care of yourself. Crafting a life's work is a marathon, not a sprint. Make sure to take time for yourself and to recharge. Don't be afraid to ask for help when you need it.

Creating a living out of your passion is a challenging but rewarding journey. With dedication, hard work, and a willingness to take risks, you can turn your passion into a career. Take the time to identify your passion, research the industry, and develop a plan to pursue your goals. It is also important to be flexible and adapt to changes along the way, as success may not always come in the way you expect it to. Above all, believe in yourself and your abilities, and never give up on your dreams. With perseverance and determination, you can turn your passion into a fulfilling and successful career. And always remember to take care of yourself and prioritize self-care, as this will help you stay motivated, focused, and energized along the way.

"The way to finding your passion is to follow your heart."

ꕥ

XIII

Cultivating Your Creative Side Nurturing Your Passions

Nurturing your creative side and cultivating your passions is essential to discovering your life's purpose. It can be difficult to find the motivation to pursue your passions, but it is worth the effort. With the right mindset and dedication, you can unlock your creative potential and find your true purpose.

The first step to cultivating your creative side is to identify your passions. Take some time to reflect on what you enjoy doing and what makes you feel fulfilled. Think about activities that bring you joy and make you feel alive. Once you have identified your passions, it is important to make time for them. Schedule time in your day to pursue your passions and make sure to stick to it.

The next step is to find ways to express your creativity. This could be through writing, painting, drawing, photography, or any other creative outlet. Experiment with different mediums and find what works best for you. Don't be afraid to try something new and take risks. You never know what you might discover.

It is also important to find a supportive community. Surround yourself with people who share your passions and can help you grow. This could be a group of friends, a mentor, or an online community. Having a support system will help you stay motivated and inspired.

Finally, don't be afraid to make mistakes. Mistakes are part of the creative process and can help you learn and grow. Don't be too hard on yourself and remember that failure is part of the journey.

Cultivating your creative side and nurturing your passions is essential to discovering your life's purpose. With the right mindset and dedication, you can unlock your creative potential and find your true purpose. Take the time to identify your passions, make time for them, express your creativity, find a supportive community, and don't be afraid to make mistakes. With these steps, you can start your journey to finding your passion and living a life of purpose.

"Your passion is the wind that propels you towards your dreams."

ঌ

XIV

Passion and Purpose How They Work Together

Passion and purpose are two of the most powerful forces that drive us to achieve our goals and live our best lives. When we combine them, we can unlock our full potential and create a life of meaning and fulfillment.

Passion is the spark that ignites our drive and ambition. It is the fire that fuels our desire to achieve our goals and live our best lives. Passion is the energy that propels us forward and gives us the courage to take risks and try new things. It is the enthusiasm that keeps us motivated and inspired.

Purpose is the direction that passion takes us. It is the reason why we do what we do. Purpose gives us focus and clarity, and it helps us stay on track and stay motivated. It is the compass that guides us and helps us make decisions that are in line with our values and goals.

When we combine passion and purpose, we can create a powerful synergy that helps us reach our goals and live our best lives. Passion gives us the energy and enthusiasm to pursue our goals, while purpose gives us the focus and direction to stay on track. Together, they can help us create a life of meaning and fulfillment.

Passion and purpose are like two sides of the same coin. They work together to help us reach our goals and live our best lives. When we combine them, we can unlock our full potential and create a life of meaning and fulfillment. With passion and purpose, we can achieve anything we set our minds to.

Indeed, passion and purpose are important elements of a fulfilling and successful life. Passion gives us the drive and motivation to pursue our goals, while purpose provides a sense of direction and meaning. When we align our passions with our values and beliefs, we can create a life that is truly authentic and fulfilling. Additionally, combining passion and purpose helps us to stay motivated and engaged, even when faced with challenges or setbacks. It is important to continuously reflect on our passions and purpose and make sure that they are aligned with our life goals and values. With this powerful combination, we can create a life of happiness and fulfillment, and achieve our dreams.

"The road to discovering your passion starts with believing in yourself."

ꕥ

XV

The Power of Passion Making a Difference in the World

Passion is a powerful force that can make a difference in the world. It can be the driving force behind achieving great things, inspiring others, and creating positive change.

Passion is a strong emotion that can be used to fuel our actions and propel us forward. It can be the spark that ignites our creativity and motivates us to take action. Passion can be the driving force behind achieving our goals and making a difference in the world. It can be the source of inspiration that helps us to stay focused and motivated, even when the going gets tough.

When we are passionate about something, we are more

likely to take risks and push ourselves to do things that we may not have done otherwise. Passion can be the catalyst for positive change, as it can inspire us to take action and make a difference in the world. Passion can also be the source of motivation that helps us to stay focused and committed to our goals.

Passion can also be the source of inspiration for others. When we are passionate about something, we can inspire others to take action and make a difference in the world. We can be a source of encouragement and support for those around us, helping them to stay motivated and focused on their goals.

Passion can also be the source of strength and resilience. When we are passionate about something, we are more likely to persevere and stay committed to our goals, even when the going gets tough. Passion can be the source of courage and determination that helps us to keep going, even when the odds are against us.

Passion is a powerful force that can make a difference in the world. It can be the driving force behind achieving great things, inspiring others, and creating positive change. By tapping into our passion and using it to drive our actions and decisions, we can create meaningful and impactful outcomes. Passion gives us the energy and drive to overcome obstacles and challenges, and to keep pushing forward towards our goals. It is a key factor in personal growth and development, and can help us to achieve our full potential. Furthermore, passion is contagious, and when we are passionate about something, it inspires others to be passionate and motivated as well. By embracing our passions and using them to make a difference, we can create a life that is fulfilling, meaningful, and positively impactful.

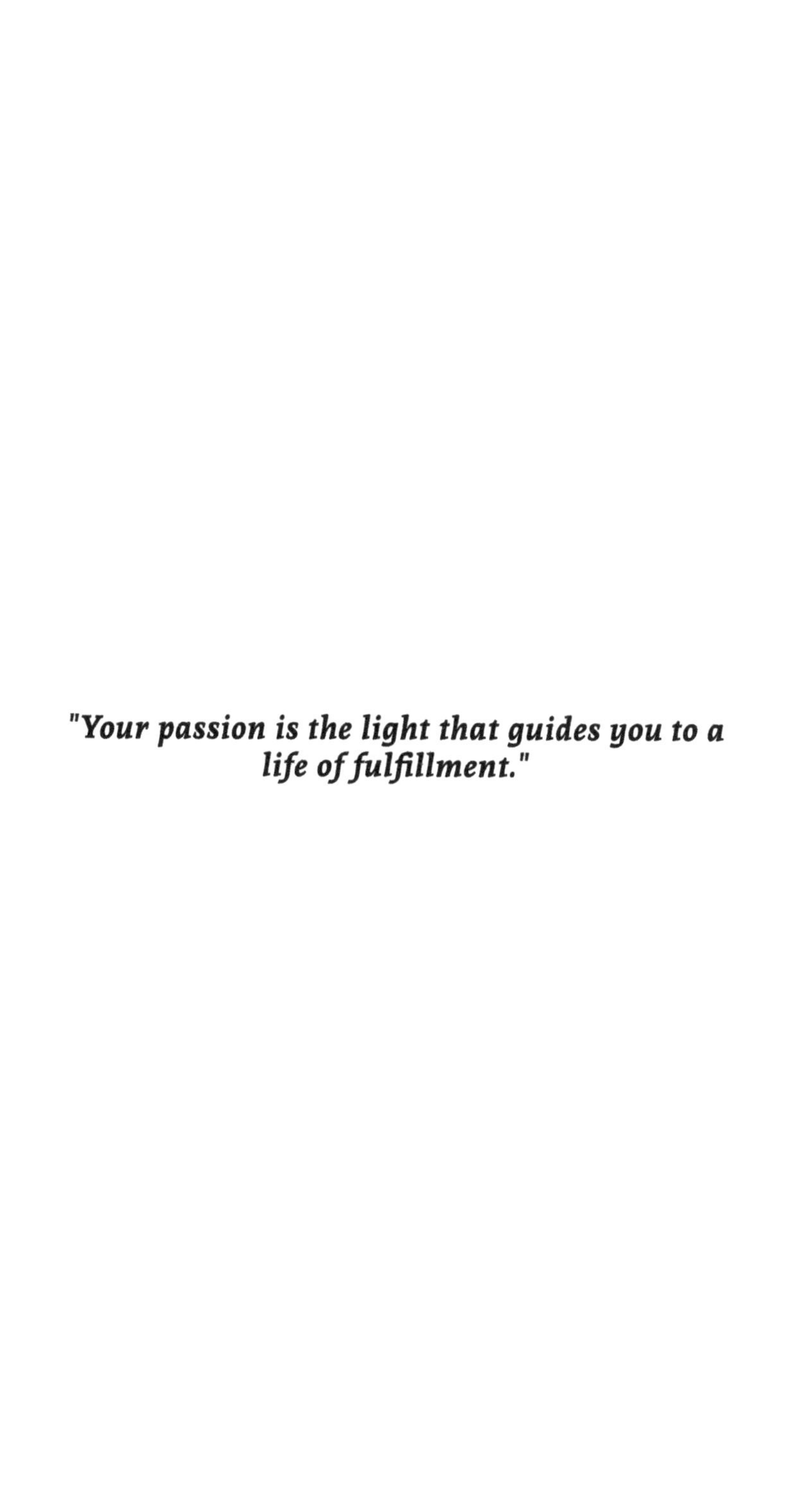

"Your passion is the light that guides you to a life of fulfillment."

Other Books Of The Author

1. The Moments When I Met God
2. Kashiyile Theertha Pathangal
3. GURU GYAN VANI
4. Abhiprerak Gita
5. ASSI SE JAIN GHAT TAK
6. Hopelessness of Arjuna
7. The Soul and It's True Nature
8. Sense of Action (Karma)
9. Action through Wisdom
10. Action through Wisdom
11. THEORY AND PRACTICAL OF EVERY ACTION
12. LOGICAL UNDERSTANDING OF THE SUPREME
13. THE IMPERISHABLE SUPREME
14. Yatra Nishadraj se Hanuman Ghat Tak
15. Yatra Karnatak Ghat se Raja Ghat Tak
16. Yatra Pandey Ghat se Prayagraj Ghat Tak
17. Yatra Ranjendra Prasad Ghat se Dattatreya Ghat Tak
18. YaatraSindhiya Ghat se Gwaliar Ghat Tak
19. Yatra Mangala Gauri Ghat se Hanuman Gadhi Ghat Tak
20. Yatra Gaay Ghat Se Nishad Ghat Tak
21. MAA GANGA, GHATEN EVM UTSAV
22. Ganga Arti Dev Deepavali evam Any Utsav
23. Potentials of Digitalized India
24. VEDIC CONSCIOUSNESS
25. A Brief Introduction to Vedic Science
26. Kashi ke Barah Jyotirling
27. IMPACT OF MOTIVATION
28. Let's have a Milky Way Journey
29. Color Therapy in a Nutshell

30. Rigveda in a Nutshell
31. Yajurveda in a Nutshell
32. Samveda in a Nutshell
33. Atharva Veda in a Nutshell
34. Ayushman Bhava - Ayurveda
35. Srimad Bhagavad Gita and Upanishad Connection
36. Srimad Bhagavad Gita - an attempt to summarize each chapter.
37. Facts and Impact of Nakshatra
38. Astro Gems - NAVARATNA
39. Ekadashi - A Concise Overview
40. A Concise View of Hanuman Chalisa
41. Inspirational Gita
42. Nakshatraranyam
43. Summary of 18 Mahapuranas
44. Synopsis of 18 Upa Puranas
45. Rigvediya Upanishads
46. Shukla Yajurvediya Upanishads
47. Krishna Yajurvediya Upanishads
48. Samavediya Upanishads
49. Atharvavediya Upanishads
50. The Seven Great Sages
51. From Rocket Scientist to President Dr. APJ Abdul Kalam
52. The Visionary's Voice - Quotes of Dr. APJ Abdul Kalam
53. The Wisdom of Swami Vivekananda: Insights and Inspiration from a Legendary Spiritual Teacher
54. Ayurvedic Remedies from the Garden
55. Sages and Seers
56. Rising Strong – Motivational Stories of Women
57. Beyond Flames -Mystery stories of Funeral Ghat Manikarnika
58. The Origins of Tulsi: A Look at the Mythological Roots of the Plant"

59. The Holistic Cow: A Look at the Physical, Spiritual, and Cultural Importance of Cows in India
60. Arts of Healing
61. Exploring the Divine
62. Understanding Five Elements
63. The Etymology of Ram
64. Symbols of India
65. Voice of Change (About Speeches of Great Men)
66. She Speaks (About Speeches of Great Women)
67. Patriotism on Celluloid – Brief About Patriotic Films
68. The Music of Motivation: A Brief Guide to Inspirational Film Songs
69. **Unlocking the Secrets of the Dashopanishads**
70. A Cultural Mosaic
71. Ancient Traditions, Modern Minds
72. Ecos of Ancient Wisdom
73. Beneath the Surface
74. From Temples to Ashrams
75. Sages of the Subcontinent
76. The Art of Healling (Ayurveda, Yoga & Naturopathy)
77. Indian Kitchen
78. The Festivals of India
79. The Indian Epics Retold
80. The Power of Mantras
81. The Indian River Ganges
82. The Indian Architecture
83. Rites of Passage
84. The Indian Silk Road
85. The Indian Literature
86. The Indian Villages
87. The Indian Folks & Crafts
88. The Way of Buddha
89. The Ramayan of Tulsidas

90. Astrological Remedies
91. The Secret Power of Motivation
92. Secret of Developing your Inner Strength
93. The Secret Path to Motivation
94. The Art and Secret of Positive Thinking
95. The Secrets of Practicing Ethical Living
96. Indian Art and Painting
97. The Indian Herbalism
98. Bharatanatyam to Kathak
99. Exploring India's Astrological Remedies
100. The Indian Festival of Flowers
101. Indian Handicrafts
102. The Splashes of Joy – India's Colour Festival
103. The Indian Science of Astrology
104. The Indian Mythology
105. Path to Enlightenment
106. The Indian Spirituality for Children
107. Aromas of India
108. The Secrets of Healthy Relationships
109. Ancestral Ties
110. The Indian Street Food
111. Discovering America
112. The Indian Textile
113. Listening to Motivational Speeches
114. Taste of India
115. A Cultural Journey through Indian Nuptials
116. Motivational Quote for Change
117. Secret Strategies for Making Money
118. Secrets to Cultivate a Positive Mindset
119. A Tapestry of Cultures: Exploring India from Kashmir to Kanyakumari
120. Achieving Your Dreams with Resilience: Secret Strategies for Overcoming Obstacles

121. Innovative Startups - 25 Startup Ideas to Spark Your Business Creativity
122. Export Management: Strategies for Global Success
123. Exporting from India - A Step by Step Guide
124. Finance Fundamentals: Mastering Financial Management for Business Success
125. Global Growth Strategies for International Business Development
126. Marketing Mastery: Unlocking the Secrets of Modern Marketing
127. Operations Mastery: Managing the Flow of Value in Business
128. Strategic Business Management: Navigating the Modern Business Landscape
129. Human Resource Management Strategies for Building and Managing a High Performance Team
130. The Indian Landscapes and Nature: An Exploration Of India's Natural Beauty And Diversity
131. The Indian Street Performances: A Cultural Exploration of India's Street Performances
132. Affirming Your Self-Worth: Strategies for Achieving Emotional Wellbeing
133. Cultivating Self-Discipline: Secrets Methods for Achieving Your Goals
134. Embracing Change: Strategies for Adapting to Life's Challenges
135. Embracing Your Uniqueness: Secret Strategies for Living an Authentic Life
136. Finding Motivation in Despondency: Coping with Difficult Times
137. Embracing Change
138. Learning to Love Yourself
139. Managing Time for Yourself

140. Unlock the keys to Self-Motivation
141. Secret to Boost Confidence
142. Unlocking your Potential: A Path to Inner-strength & Success
143. Secrets to Develop Authentic Relationship
144. Secrets to Build a Successful Career
145. Secrets to Live with Gratitude
146. Secrets to Create a Life of Abundance
147. Secrets to Cultivate Self-Awareness
148. The Power of Helping Hands
149. Finding Your Passion
150. The Indian Mythical Creatures
151. The Indian Women Saints
152. The Wisdom of the Saints
153. "The Indian Royalty: A Cultural and Historical Exploration of India's Maharajas and their kingdom"
154. The Mystic Land: A Cultural and Spiritual Exploration of India"

CONTACT

DR. JAGADEESH PILLAI

MBA & PhD in Vedic Science

Four Times Guinness World Record Holder

Winner of Mahatma Gandhi Vishwa Shanti Puraskar and Global Peace Ambassador

Gemology, Astro & Vastu Consultant - Spiritual Counselor

Consultant for designing World Record Ideas

Efficient Tarot Card Reader

9839093003

myrichindia@gmail.com

drjagadeeshpillai@facebook

drjagadeeshpillai@instagram
jagadeeshpillai@youtube

www. JAGADEESHPILLAI.com

|| LOKAHA SAMASTHAHA SUKHINO BHAVANTU ||

ജ

Printed by Libri Plureos GmbH in Hamburg,
Germany